T0400788

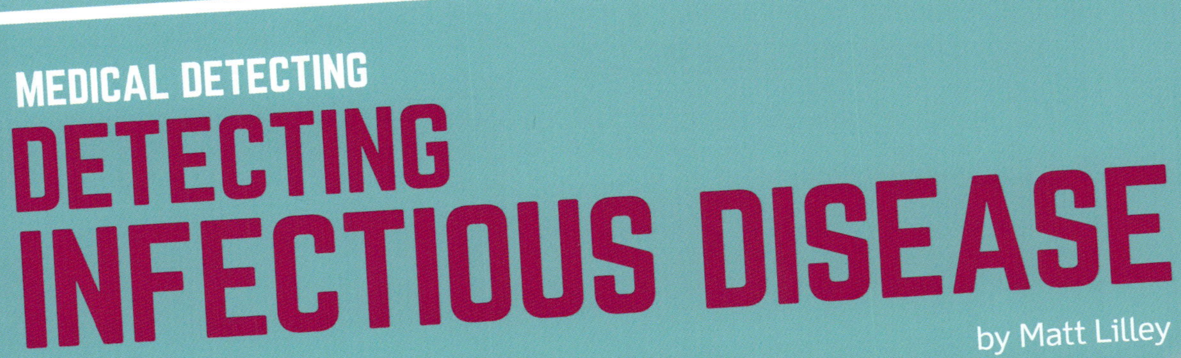

MEDICAL DETECTING

DETECTING INFECTIOUS DISEASE

by Matt Lilley

FOCUS READERS
NAVIGATOR

WWW.FOCUSREADERS.COM

Focus Readers is distributed by North Star Editions:
sales@northstareditions.com | 888-417-0195

Produced for Focus Readers by Red Line Editorial.

Content Consultant: Stephanie I. Fraley, PhD, Associate Professor of Bioengineering at the University of California, San Diego

Photographs ©: Shutterstock Images, cover, 1, 4–5, 8–9, 11, 13, 14–15, 17, 18, 20–21, 23, 25, 26–27; iStockphoto, 7, 29

Library of Congress Cataloging-in-Publication Data
Names: Lilley, Matt, author.
Title: Detecting infectious disease / by Matt Lilley.
Description: Lake Elmo, MN : Focus Readers, [2024] | Series: Medical detecting | Includes bibliographical references and index. | Audience: Grades 4-6
Identifiers: LCCN 2022058835 (print) | LCCN 2022058836 (ebook) | ISBN 9781637396261 (hardcover) | ISBN 9781637396834 (paperback) | ISBN 9781637397923 (pdf) | ISBN 9781637397404 (ebook)
Subjects: LCSH: Communicable diseases--Diagnosis--Juvenile literature.
Classification: LCC RC113.3 .L55 2024 (print) | LCC RC113.3 (ebook) | DDC 616.9/0475--dc23/eng/20221223
LC record available at https://lccn.loc.gov/2022058835
LC ebook record available at https://lccn.loc.gov/2022058836

Printed in the United States of America
Mankato, MN
082023

ABOUT THE AUTHOR

Matt Lilley has written 20 nonfiction children's books. He also has an MS in scientific and technical writing. The focus of his degree was on health writing for kids. He loves researching and writing about all sorts of topics. He lives in Minnesota with his family.

TABLE OF CONTENTS

CHAPTER 1

A SORE THROAT

A girl has a sore throat and a bad cough. She has a runny nose, too. These are **symptoms** of an illness. The girl might have a cold. Or it might be something worse. It could be strep throat or COVID-19. Her doctor wants to know for sure.

Doctors sometimes use tools to hold down the tongues of their patients. Then they can look at their patients' throats.

Strep throat is caused by **bacteria**. If the girl has strep, the doctor can give her antibiotics. Antibiotics kill bacteria. However, COVID-19 is caused by a **virus**. Antibiotics don't work against viruses.

The doctor looks at her throat. It is red. First, he tests for strep. He swabs the back of the girl's throat. The swab collects a sample. Next, the doctor does a COVID-19 test. He swabs her nostrils.

The test results come quickly. The doctor looks at them. The strep test is negative. But the second test is positive. The girl has COVID-19.

The doctor tells the girl to go home and rest. COVID-19 is an **infectious**

Doctors give advice and directions to their patients after they figure out the problem.

disease, so she should avoid other people. He also says that she should wash her hands often and wear masks. So should others around her. The doctor expects the girl to feel better in several days. She can go back to school when she is no longer infectious.

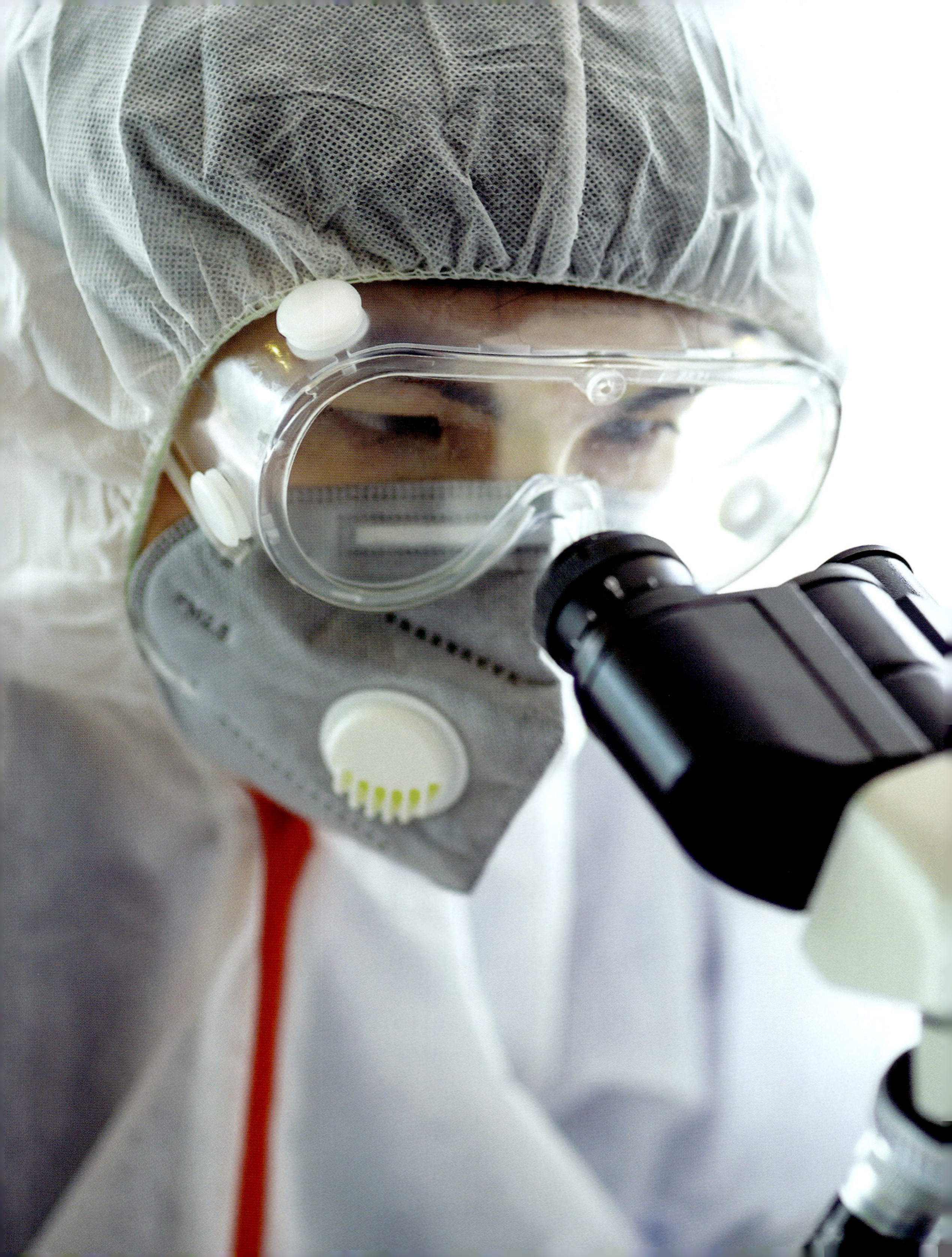

CHAPTER 2

DETECTION HISTORY

Infectious diseases are caused by tiny germs such as viruses and bacteria. Germs can make people sick. Then sick people can spread the germs to others.

In ancient times, doctors didn't understand how diseases spread. They only knew that some sicknesses spread between people. Then, in the 1340s,

The organisms that cause infectious diseases are tiny. Sometimes scientists need microscopes to see them.

a **contagious** disease called the Black Death struck Europe. People didn't know how to stop it. Millions of people died.

Later, in the 1850s, England had a cholera **epidemic**. Cholera is a sickness that causes diarrhea. One doctor thought cholera spread through water. He made a map of the water pumps and houses

BAD AIR?

In the 1300s, many people thought the Black Death was caused by "bad air." People tried to change how the air smelled. They used fire, smoke, herbs, and wax. One doctor even thought the smell of a goat would help. However, none of these things worked. The Black Death kept spreading.

Some medieval doctors wore masks shaped like beaks. The masks sometimes had scents inside.

of victims in one town. He thought that closing a central water pump could end the **outbreak**. It worked. He had detected the source of the disease.

People had used microscopes to see bacteria since the late 1600s. Then, in the 1930s, scientists invented electron microscopes. Scientists could finally see viruses. Later, scientists made tests to detect bits of germs. The germs could be signs of sickness.

GERM THEORY

Germ theory is the idea that germs cause infectious diseases. In the 1800s, some scientists accepted germ theory. But others didn't. So, a scientist named Robert Koch did an experiment. He was studying anthrax. This deadly disease can infect animals and people.

After some cows died of anthrax, Koch looked at their blood. Using a microscope, he saw rod-shaped bacteria in the blood. Koch thought these bacteria caused anthrax. He grew more of the bacteria. Then he gave the bacteria to healthy mice. The mice got anthrax. Koch looked at the mice's blood. It had the same rod-shaped bacteria.

Koch's work impressed many scientists. It helped them accept germ theory. Koch had proved that a specific germ could cause a specific

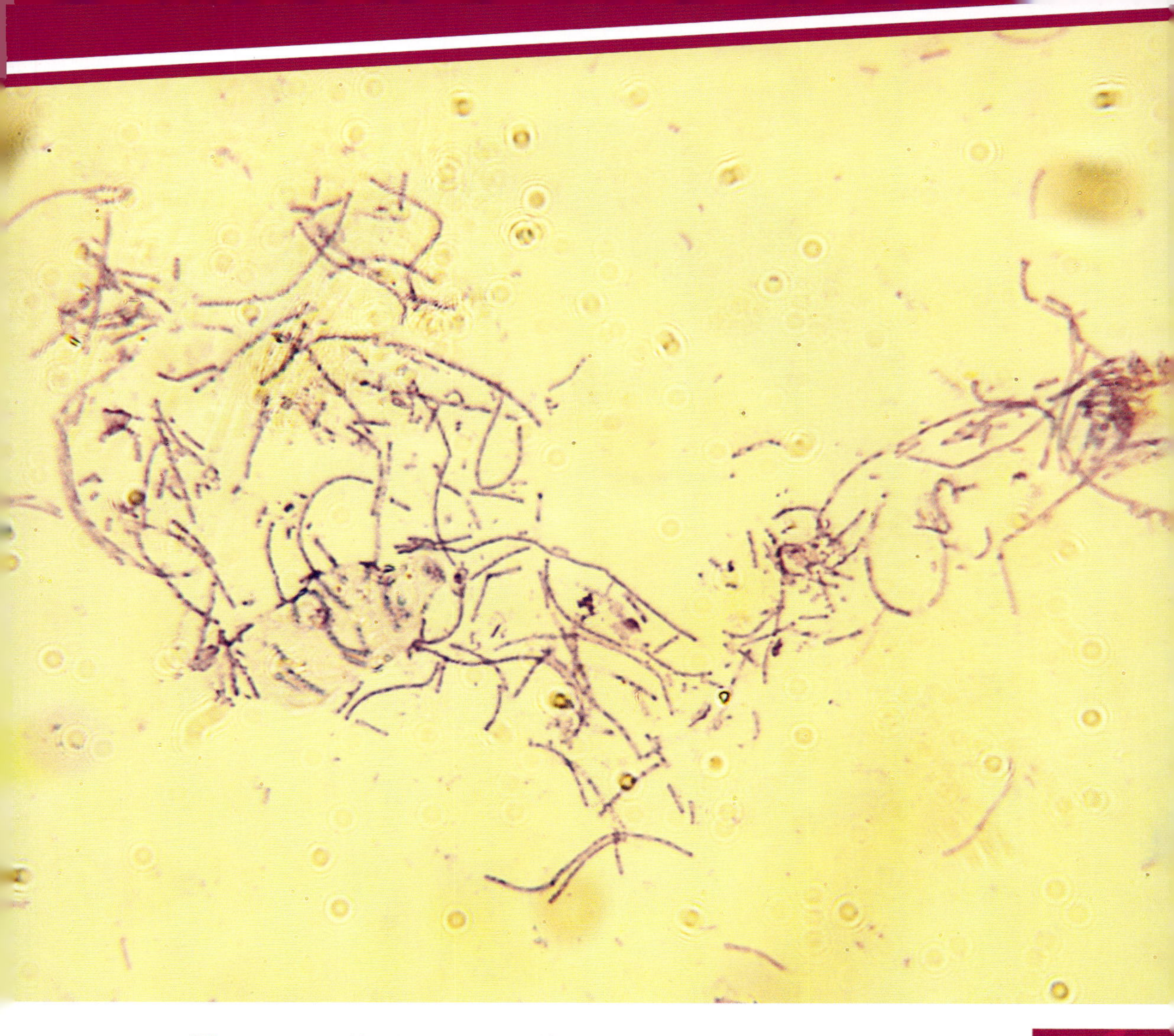

The germs that cause anthrax can be seen under a microscope. They look like chains of rod-shaped bacteria.

disease. Later, Koch did experiments with other diseases, too. His work led to discoveries about cholera and tuberculosis.

CHAPTER 3

DETECTION IN INDIVIDUALS

Modern doctors have many ways to detect infectious diseases. Most often, they use lab tests. Sometimes doctors take samples from the nose. Sometimes they take samples from the throat or other areas. That is because different infections show up in different parts of the body.

Many lab tests use samples from the nose. COVID-19 tests are one example.

Some lab tests use a tool called a culture. To do a culture, a doctor collects a sample from a patient. The sample has germs in it. The doctor tries to make the germs grow. That way, the doctor can identify the harmful bacteria.

Another kind of test is a stain. To do a stain, a scientist puts a sample on a microscope slide. Then, the scientist puts liquids on the slide. Different types of bacteria show up with different colors and shapes. Then, scientists can identify diseases.

A PCR test is different. It copies **DNA** material from a sample. That makes it easier to detect disease-causing germs.

Machines help copy DNA from samples for PCR tests.

A PCR test is very accurate. But it takes a few hours to get results.

Another kind of test is an antigen test. All viruses have pieces called antigens. Every virus's antigen has a different shape. An antigen test detects that piece. Antigen tests can give results in just a few minutes.

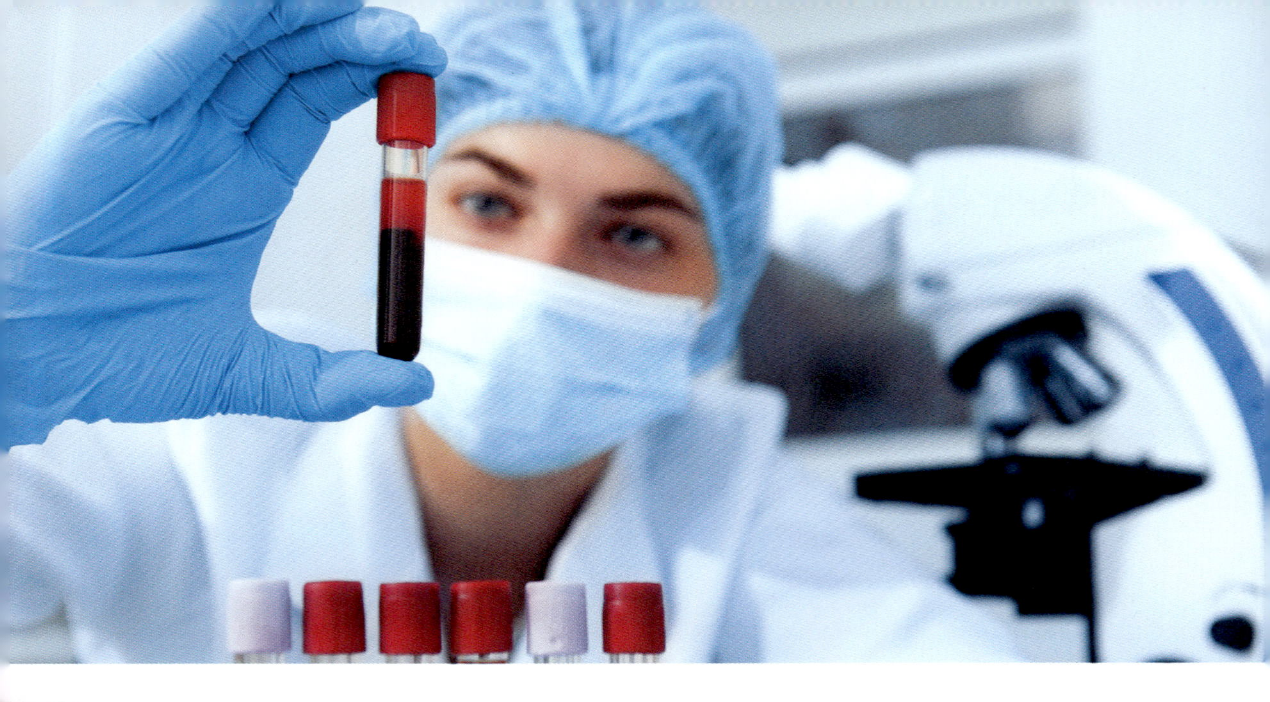

Scientists can use blood samples to do antibody tests.

An antibody test is another type. If a person's body notices a disease, it makes antibodies to fight the sickness. Antibodies fit together with germ antigens. Antigens have unique shapes, so antibodies do, too. An antibody test detects if someone has antibodies to a virus.

Each of these tests can be helpful. But they aren't perfect. Cultures can take days or weeks. Stains don't show the exact type of bacteria. PCR and antibody tests might give positive results after patients are better. And antigen tests are not always accurate.

DETECTION IN ANIMALS

Sometimes sickness spreads between people and animals. Symptoms in animals can be similar to symptoms in people. For example, a pig with swine flu might cough. It might have a fever. It might sneeze. Scientists can test animals for sickness. Tests for animals are similar to tests for people. Scientists can take samples and find out what the sicknesses are.

CHAPTER 4

DETECTION IN POPULATIONS

Scientists have ways to slow infectious diseases in large populations. The basic steps are test, trace, and isolate. First, scientists test sick people. This identifies the sickness. Next, scientists trace where the disease has gone. Infections spread, so it is important to find the source. The last step is to isolate.

Phones can help trace diseases in populations. They can track where infected people went and which other people they met.

That means cutting off the source from other people. People who have been exposed to diseases may have to **quarantine**.

Doctors used this three-step method with COVID-19. In December 2019, people in Wuhan, China, started getting sick. Doctors didn't know why. They tested samples from sick people's lungs. Soon, they identified the virus that caused the sickness. Then, doctors tried to trace where it came from. Many viruses start from bats. This time, scientists weren't sure. They tested many ideas.

The next step was to isolate. But COVID-19 had already spread in China.

Using hand sanitizer can help slow the spread of infectious diseases between people.

It was too late to stop the virus. Some other countries were able to isolate. For example, South Korea used the "test, trace, isolate" method with strict rules. The country also encouraged actions such as handwashing and wearing masks. Those are important actions to take for any infectious disease. Sick people and those who are not sick can do them. These decisions helped South Korea slow the spread of COVID-19 in the country.

GLOBAL DETECTION AND REPORTING

The World Health Organization (WHO) tries to detect new disease outbreaks around the world. When there is an outbreak, information needs to spread fast. But an outbreak might start somewhere without phone or internet access. It can be hard to communicate. So, the WHO sends kits. They have equipment like phones and chargers. Then doctors can detect and report on diseases.

People of different ages can help slow the spread of infectious diseases.

Scientists can also use sewage to detect infectious disease. They get samples from wastewater treatment plants. Then they test them. Some scientists did this for COVID-19. Finding more of the virus in sewage means more people in the area have it.

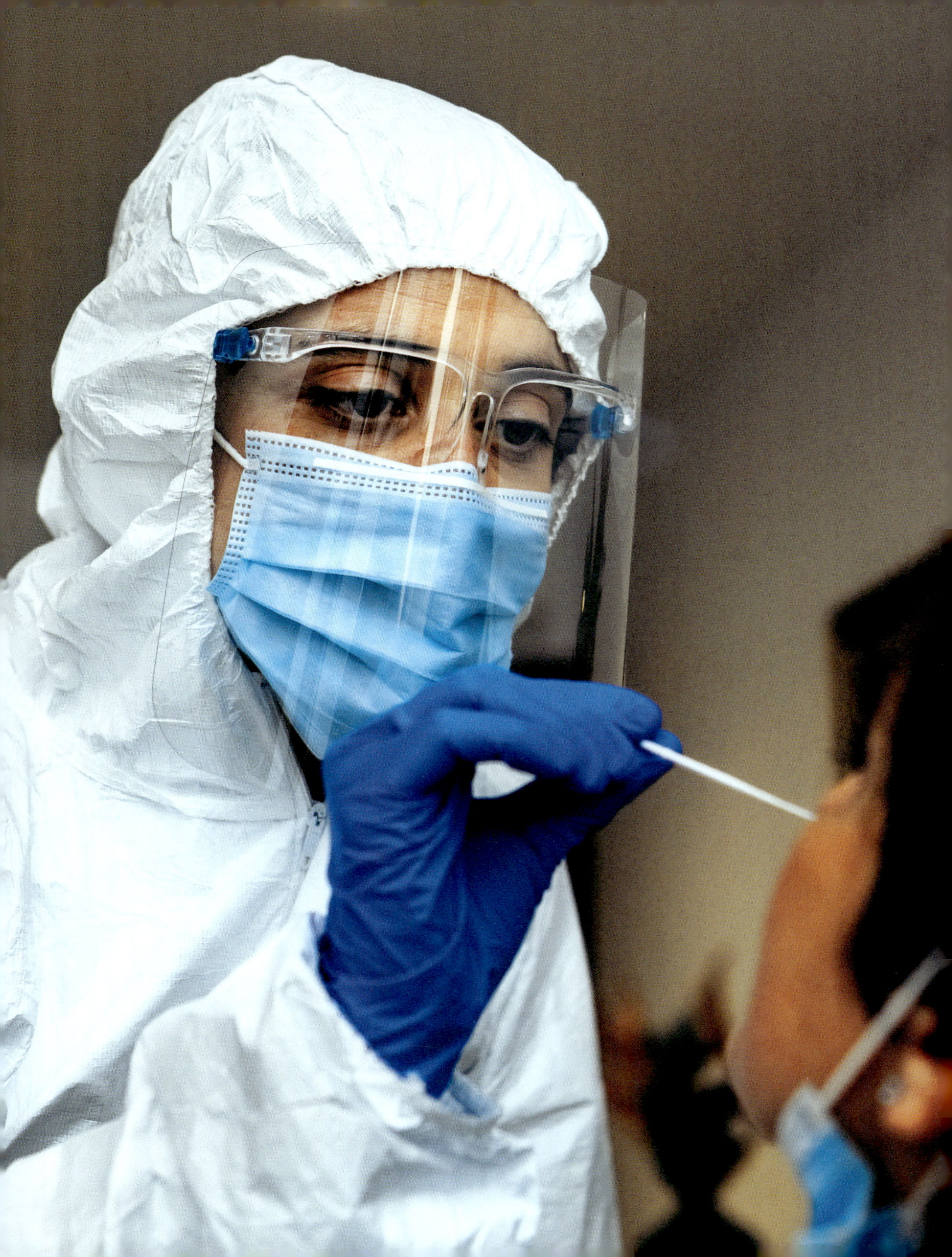

CHAPTER 5

BEFORE IT SPREADS

When new diseases show up, quick detection is important. After doctors notice people getting sick, it might take only a few weeks to identify the virus. But that can be too slow. If doctors can detect it faster, they might be able to stop it.

Scientists want new ways to detect diseases like COVID-19 before they

Doctors often wear gloves, masks, and goggles when they test for infectious diseases. That helps them avoid getting the diseases.

spread. So, some scientists are working on new kinds of PCR tests. They would give faster results. Scientists want to make tests cheaper, too.

Scientists also began working on a device to find viruses in the air. It would shoot viruses with a laser. The laser would make them vibrate. Different viruses vibrate in different ways. The device could help monitor the presence of viruses in public places.

Many diseases also spread from animals. So, companies began working on devices that can read the DNA of different germs. These devices would be cheap and easy to use, too.

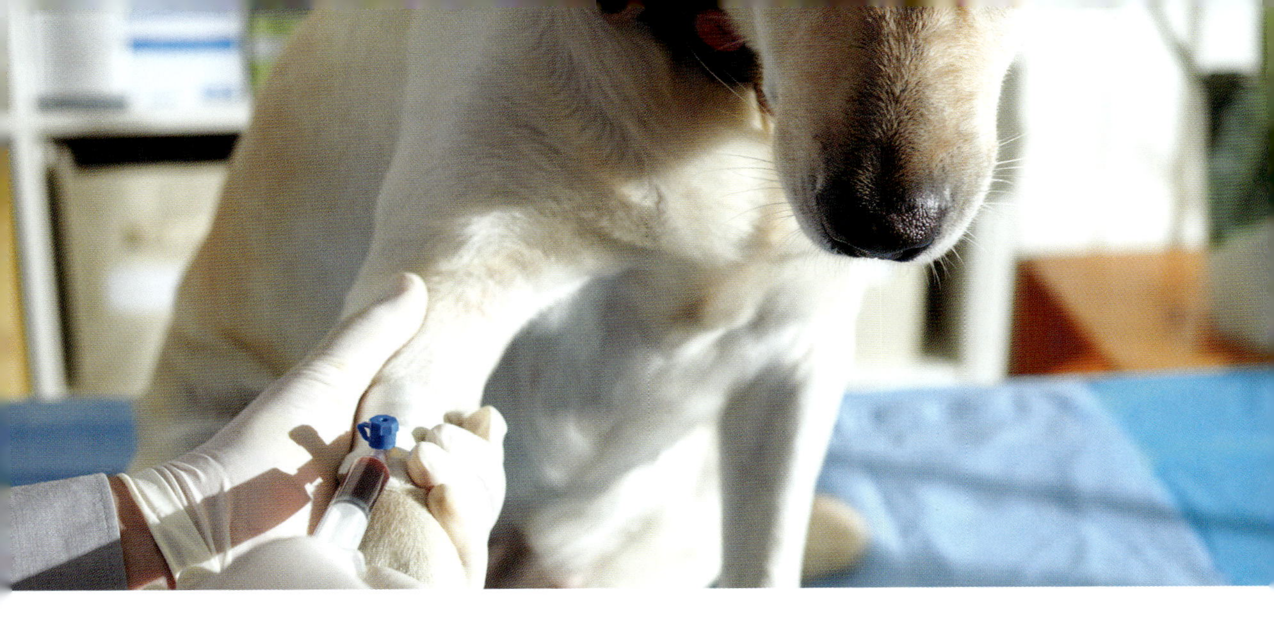

Veterinarians can use blood testing to check for some diseases in animals.

In the future, single-virus tracking could also help slow disease spread. That's when scientists tag a virus with dye. With a microscope, they watch the virus infect a living cell. This helps scientists learn how viruses infect cells. Then, scientists can use that information. They can discover new ways to prevent infection.

FOCUS ON

DETECTING INFECTIOUS DISEASE

Write your answers on a separate piece of paper.

1. Write a paragraph that describes the main ideas of Chapter 4.

2. Suppose a student has a runny nose and sore throat. What should the student do before going to school? Why?

3. What is the correct order for the steps to stop infectious diseases in populations?

- **A.** isolate, test, trace
- **B.** trace, test, isolate
- **C.** test, trace, isolate

4. Many infectious diseases spread through people. Where would it be the most difficult to stop the spread of an infectious disease?

- **A.** a crowded city
- **B.** a small town
- **C.** a rural area

Answer key on page 32.

GLOSSARY

bacteria

Microscopic, single-celled living things. Some bacteria cause disease, and some do not.

contagious

Able to spread to other people.

DNA

The genetic material in the cells of living organisms.

epidemic

When an infectious disease spreads to a large group of people in a population.

infectious

Likely to spread sickness.

outbreak

When an infectious disease suddenly starts spreading.

quarantine

To stay alone for a period of time in order to prevent sickness from spreading.

symptoms

Signs of an illness or disease.

virus

A tiny substance that can cause illness in people and animals.

TO LEARN MORE

BOOKS

Krasner, Barbara. *Bubonic Plague: How the Black Death Changed History*. North Mankato, MN: Capstone Press, 2019.

London, Martha. *Flattening the Curve*. Minneapolis: Abdo, 2021.

Sommer, Nathan. *The Coronavirus Pandemic*. Minneapolis: Bellwether Media, 2022.

NOTE TO EDUCATORS

Visit **www.focusreaders.com** to find lesson plans, activities, links, and other resources related to this title.

INDEX

Answer Key: 1. Answers will vary; **2.** Answers will vary; **3.** C; **4.** A